For

Sandra

1993

To my family and friends,
whose love carried me through

Copyright © 1991
Peter Pauper Press, Inc.
202 Mamaroneck Avenue
White Plains, New York 10601
ISBN 0-88088-743-5
Printed in Hong Kong
7   6   5   4

THANKS

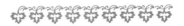

The greatest gift of life is friendship and I have received it.

Hubert Humphrey

Peace is not God's gift to his creatures. It is our gift—to each other.

Elie Wiesel

If one cares to send the very best, one flies home for Thanksgiving.

Walter Shapiro

Thank you, but I have other plans.

Paul Fussell,
suggested reply to
"Have a nice day"

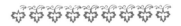

Gratitude is the sign of noble souls.

Aesop

Whenever I get full of myself and think I'm a star, I think about the nice elderly couple who approached me with a camera on a street in Honolulu one day. When I struck a pose for them, the man said, "No, no, we want you to take a picture of *us*." Things like that are very good for me.

Tom Selleck

We hope that, when the
insects take over the world,
they will remember with
gratitude how we took them
along on all our picnics.

Bill Vaughan

Kind hearts are the garden,
Kind thoughts are the roots,
Kind words are the blossoms,
Kind deeds are the fruit.

John Ruskin

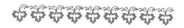

I wanted to live very much. I wanted to be around the people I loved and to be out of intensive care. So I let them do the open-lung biopsy, and I went on life support, which helped me to recover my strength. I remember passing the crucial time. I was still in intensive care and still had a fever of 105 and was slightly out of my mind. But I remember saying, "Thank you, God."

Elizabeth Taylor

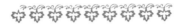

If you want to live a long time
you have to smoke cigars,
drink martinis and dance
close.

George Burns

Chili's a lot like sex: When it's
good it's great, and even when
it's bad, it's not so bad.

Bill Boldenweck

Friends are born, not made.

Henry Adams

The best part of the whole thing was that the President of the United States called me "Hot Stuff."

Beverly Sills,
at the 8th annual
Kennedy Center gala

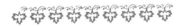

My fan mail is enormous.
Everyone is under six.

Alexander Calder

One of life's gifts is that each
of us, no matter how tired and
downtrodden, finds reasons
for thankfulness: for the crops
carried in from the fields and
the grapes from the vineyard.

J. Robert Moskin

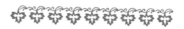

I'd like to thank Larry Bird for having a slightly off year and letting me win the award.

Earvin "Magic" Johnson,
on being named
Most Valuable Player

God is Not Dead. He is Alive and Playing for the Mets.

Sign on statue of
George Washington on
Wall Street when 1969 "miracle"
N. Y. Mets won World Series

To my mother, who bought me my first guitar, and to my sister, who is my best critic, my best audience, and my best friend.

Tracy Chapman,
Thank you's
at Grammy Awards

O thou who has given us so much, mercifully grant us one thing more—a grateful heart.

George Herbert

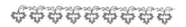

Too much of a good thing is simply wonderful.

Liberace

I am reminded of the North Dakota farmer who went out to the barn one morning when it was about forty degrees below zero. He sat down on a milk stool and took hold of the animal. She turned to him and said, "Thanks for the warm hand."

Everett M. Dirksen

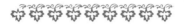

I have a sense of humor about the shoe situation. It helped me in the end. When they opened the closet, the nice part was they found shoes, but thank God there were no skeletons.

Imelda Marcos

Kindness is a language the dumb can speak and the deaf can hear and understand.

Christian Bovee

I don't look for perfection any
more. Right now is perfection.
I don't have to be the best or
the biggest any more. The
greatest joy is appreciation.
Once you have something in
life and almost lose it and
manage to get it back, you
learn about appreciation.

Sid Caesar

Happy the man who finds a
generous friend.

Greek Proverb

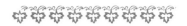

Thanks for the last time we
were together.

Danish Greeting

Gratitude is the fairest blossom
which springs from the soul;
and the heart of man knoweth
none more fragrant.

Hosea Ballou

America! America!
God shed His grace on thee
And crown thy good with
    brotherhood
From sea to shining sea!
> *Katherine Lee Bates,*
> America the Beautiful

A man is occasionally thankful
when he says "thank you."
> *Benjamin Disraeli*

I was the best I ever had.

Woody Allen

The way to a man's heart is through his stomach.

Fanny Fern

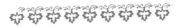

I've been in more laps than a napkin.

Mae West

The result was magnificent . . .
I became the father of two
girls and two boys, lovely
children—by good fortune
they all look like my wife.

Artur Rubinstein

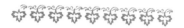

I don't deserve this award, but
I have arthritis and I don't
deserve that either.

Jack Benny

My life began with Ronnie.

Nancy Reagan

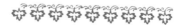

A warm smile is the universal
language of kindness.

William Arthur Ward

I feel a very unusual sensation—
it is not indigestion, I think it
must be gratitude.

Benjamin Disraeli

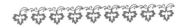

I am at my desk, having just returned from seeing a patient . . . who is alive and at the moment well because of the miracle of medical progress. In recalling her happiness and the look of fondness and gratitude she gave me, I cannot help reaching out in appreciation to those persons, some known to me and many unknown, whose efforts have permitted me this, the supreme reward to the physician.

Charles L. Hudson, M.D.

Gratitude is the rosemary of the heart.

Minna Antrim

I don't have to have millions of dollars to be happy. All I need is to have some clothes on my back, eat a decent meal when I want to, and get a little loving when I feel like it. That's the bottom line, man.

Ray Charles

I'm glad we don't have to play
in the shade.

Bobby Jones,
on being told it was
105° in the shade

Who rideth so late through
  the night-wind wild?
It is the father with his child;
He has the little one well
  in his arm;
He holds him safe, and
  he folds him warm.

Goethe

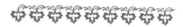

Who ran to help me when
  I fell,
And would some pretty
  story tell,
Or kiss the place to make
  it well?
  My Mother.

Ann Taylor

And though I ebb in worth, I'll
flow in thanks.

John Taylor

Thanksgiving comes to us out of the prehistoric dimness, universal to all ages and all faiths. At whatever straws we must grasp, there is always a time for gratitude and new beginnings.

J. Robert Moskin

Never Explain—your Friends do not need it and your Enemies will not believe you anyway.

Elbert Hubbard

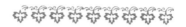

Remember God's bounty in the year. String the pearls of His favor. Hide the dark parts, except so far as they are breaking out in light! Give this one day to thanks, to joy, to gratitude!

Henry Ward Beecher

Gratitude is merely the secret hope of further favors.

François de La Rochefoucauld

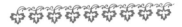

Amazing grace, how sweet
   the sound,
That saved a wretch like me.
I once was lost, but now
   I'm found.
Was blind, but now I see.

John Newton

Friend: one who knows all
about you and loves you just
the same.

Elbert Hubbard

Happy is the child whose
father died rich.

Proverb

Gratitude is a debt which
usually goes on accumulating
like blackmail; the more you
pay, the more is exacted.

Mark Twain

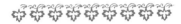

Childhood smells of perfume
and brownies.

David Leavitt,
on a son embracing
his mother

All that I am or hope to be I
owe to my mother.

Abraham Lincoln

I will praise the name of God
with a song, and will magnify
him with thanksgiving.

Psalms 69:30

A baby is God's opinion that
the world should go on.

Carl Sandburg

When we hear the baby laugh,
it is the loveliest thing that can
happen to us.

Sigmund Freud

Health is the thing that makes
you feel that now is the best
time of the year.

Franklin P. Adams

Silent gratitude isn't very
much use to anyone.

G. B. Stern

Any fool can count the seeds
in an apple. Only God can
count all the apples in one
seed.

Robert H. Schuller

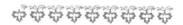

God, Who winds our sundials.

G. C. Lichtenberg

We meet this evening, not in
sorrow, but in gladness of
heart.

Abraham Lincoln,
at Civil War's end

I thank God that if I am gifted
with little of the spirit which is
said to be able to raise mortals
to the skies, I have yet none,
as I trust, of that other spirit,
which would drag angels
down.

Daniel Webster

The danger past and God
forgotten.

John Ray

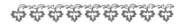

If you have a garden and a
library, you have everything
you need.

Cicero

After silence, that which
comes nearest to expressing
the inexpressible is music.

Aldous Huxley

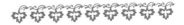

If you have lived, take
thankfully the past.

Dryden

How wealthy the gods would
be if we remembered the
promises we made when we
were in danger.

La Fontaine

Greater love hath no man
than this, that a man lay down
his life for his friends.

John 15:13

When my spirit soars, my
body falls on its knees.

G. C. Lichtenberg

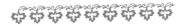

Praise the bridge that carried you over.

George Colman the Younger

Of all the things which wisdom provides to make life entirely happy, much the greatest is the possession of friendship.

Epicurus

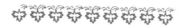

To receive honestly is the best
thanks for a good thing.

George MacDonald

As I think of the word
"friend," I recall that all the
really great things in life and
all the great impelling forces
are expressed in the simplest
words—"God," "love," "child,"
"friend."

Lyndon B. Johnson

From too much love of living,
    From hope and fear set free,
We thank with brief thanksgiving
    Whatever gods may be,
That no life lives forever,
That dead men rise up never;
That even the weariest river
    Winds somewhere safe
    to sea.

Swinburne

We love those people who
give with humility, or who
accept with ease.

Freya Stark

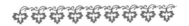

The best portion of a good man's life is his little, nameless, unremembered acts of kindness and of love.

William Wordsworth

If you want gratitude, get yourself a dog.

John V. Lindsay

One finds little ingratitude so long as one is in a position to grant favors.

French Proverb

Kind words can be short and easy to speak, but their echoes are truly endless.

Mother Teresa

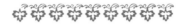

You've been reading about my bad break for weeks now. But today I think I'm the luckiest man alive. I now feel more than ever that I have much to live for.

Lou Gehrig,
terminally ill,
on "Lou Gehrig Day"
at Yankee Stadium

The best way to pay for a lovely moment is to enjoy it.
Richard Bach

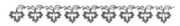

Lord most giving and
    resourceful,
I implore you;
make it your will
that this people enjoy
the goods and riches you
    naturally give,
that naturally issue from you,
that are pleasing and savory,
that delight and comfort,
though lasting but briefly,
passing away as if in a dream.

Aztec Prayer,
circa 1500's

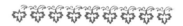

Always give your best. Never get discouraged. Never be petty. Always remember, others may hate you, but those who hate you don't win unless you hate them. And then, you destroy yourself. And so we leave, with high hopes, in good spirit and with deep humility and with very much gratefulness in our hearts.

Richard M. Nixon,
upon resigning the Presidency

How can gambling be wrong
when you win this much?

Father James Curtin,
British clergyman
who won £214,000

One can pay back the loan of
gold, but one dies forever in
debt to those who are kind.

Malayan Proverb

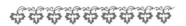

O Lord, who lends me life,
lend me a heart replete with
thankfulness.

William Shakespeare

A thankful heart is not only
the greatest virtue, but the
parent of all the other virtues.

Cicero

I thank God for my handicaps, for, through them, I have found myself, my work, and my God.

Helen Keller

We, my lords, may thank Heaven that we have something better than our brains to depend on.

Lord Chesterfield

When I'm not thank'd at all,
I'm thank'd enough,
I've done my duty, and
I've done no more.

Henry Fielding,
The Life and Death of
Tom Thumb the Great

God doesn't have to put his
name on a label in the corner
of a meadow because nobody
else makes meadows.

Cecil Laird

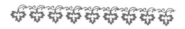

Let us be thankful for the
fools. But for them the rest of
us could not succeed.

Mark Twain

Think where man's glory most
    begins and ends,
And say my glory was I
    had such friends.

William Butler Yeats

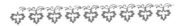

Joy untouched by thankfulness
is always suspect.

Theodor Haecker

When our perils are past, shall
our gratitude sleep?
No,—here's to the pilot that
weathered the storm!

George Canning

A man is very apt to complain
of the ingratitude of those
who have risen far above him.

Samuel Johnson

Rest and be thankful.

William Wordsworth

I don't see why I am always
asking for private, individual,
selfish miracles when every
year there are miracles like
white dogwood.

Anne Morrow Lindbergh

We have fewer friends than
we imagine, but more than we
know.

Hoffmannsthal

He who remembers the
benefits of his parents is too
much occupied with his
recollections to remember
their faults.

Pierre Jean de Béranger

Gratitude is the most exquisite
form of courtesy.

Jacques Maritain

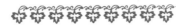

When I was young, I admired
clever people. Now that I am
old, I admire kind people.

Abraham Joshua Heschel

For turkey braised, the Lord
be praised.

From a 19th Century cookbook

Thanks are justly due for
things got without purchase.

Ovid

Gratitude is when memory is
stored in the heart and not in
the mind.

Sam N. Hampton

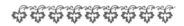

A grateful mind
By owing owes not, but still
    pays, at once
Indebted and discharg'd.
                    John Milton

Revenge is profitable, gratitude
is expensive.

                    Edward Gibbon

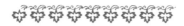

One kind word can warm
three winter months.

Japanese Proverb

They say late thanks are ever
best.

Francis Bacon

For everything that lives is
holy, life delights in life.

William Blake

God has recommended that
we should pardon injuries;
but he has not recommended
that we should pardon good
deeds.

S. R. N. Chamfort

Spring in the world!
And all things are made new.

Richard Hovey

Out of the night that covers me,
    Black as the pit from
        pole to pole,
I thank whatever gods may be
    For my unconquerable soul.

W. E. Henley

No favor can win gratitude
from a cat.

La Fontaine

Your bounty is beyond my
    speaking;
But though my mouth be
    dumb, my heart shall
    thank you.

Nicholas Rowe

He who receives a good turn should never forget it; he who does one should never remember it.

Charron

Ingratitude calls forth reproaches, as gratitude brings fresh kindnesses.

Sévigné,
letter to his daughter

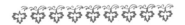

Gratitude is one of the least
articulate of the emotions,
especially when it is deep.
Felix Frankfurter

A woman drove me to drink
and I never even had the
courtesy to thank her.
W. C. Fields

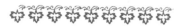

To the generous mind the heaviest debt is that of gratitude, when it is not in our power to repay it.

Benjamin Franklin

If there is anything better than to be loved, it is loving.

Anonymous

Father, we thank you, especially
for letting me fly this flight . . .
for the privilege of being able
to be in this position, to be in
this wondrous place, seeing all
these many startling, wonderful things that you have
created.
L. Gordon Cooper, Jr.,
astronaut, orbiting the earth

God has two dwellings: one in
heaven, and the other in a
meek and thankful heart.
Izaak Walton

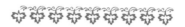

A hard man is good to find.

Mae West

I love football. I really love football. As far as I'm concerned, it's the second best thing in the world.

Joe Namath

If you want to make a
dangerous man your friend,
let him do you a favor.

Lewis E. Lawes

We have all known ingratitude;
ungrateful we have never
been.

Diane de Poitiers

These are the times that try men's souls. The Summer soldier and the sunshine patriot will, in this crisis, shrink from the service of their country, but he that stands it *now* deserves the love and thanks of man and woman.

Thomas Paine

Love beauty; it is the shadow of God on the universe.

Gabriela Mistral

Although it is a far cry from there to here, he laughed all the way.

Arthur "Bugs" Baer

This is the last of earth. I am content.

John Quincy Adams,
last words